P9-CCP-348

Beautiful BATS

Beautiful BATS

BY LINDA GLASER

Illustrated by
Sharon Lane Holm

The Millbrook Press   Brookfield, Connecticut

Ex-Library: Friends of
Lake County Public Library

LAKE COUNTY PUBLIC LIBRARY

3 3113 01719 2263

To the people at Bat Conservation International, with special
thanks to Janet Tyburec. And to Amanda Lollar whose book
The Bat in My Pocket opened my heart to bats.

LG

To my son, Michael.

SLH

Library of Congress Cataloging-in-Publication Data
Glaser, Linda.
Beautiful bats / by Linda Glaser; illustrated by Sharon Lane Holm.
p. cm.
Summary: Simple text and illustrations describe the habits and
characteristics of bats.
ISBN 0-7613-0254-9 (lib. bdg.)
1. Bats—Juvenile literature. [1. Bats.] I. Holm, Sharon Lane, ill.
II. Title.
QL737.C5G58 1997
599.4—dc21 96-48474 CIP AC

Published by The Millbrook Press
2 Old New Milford Road, Brookfield, Connecticut 06804

Copyright © 1997 by The Millbrook Press
Text copyright © 1997 by Linda Glaser
Illustrations copyright © 1997 by Sharon Lane Holm

All rights reserved
Printed in the United States of America
5 4 3 2 1

Little Brown Bats are shy, gentle animals
with strong toes and big ears and round black eyes.

On both sides of their small, furry bodies,
they have wings that open large and wide.

Their wings don't have feathers like a bird's.
Their wings have a stretchy, rubbery skin.

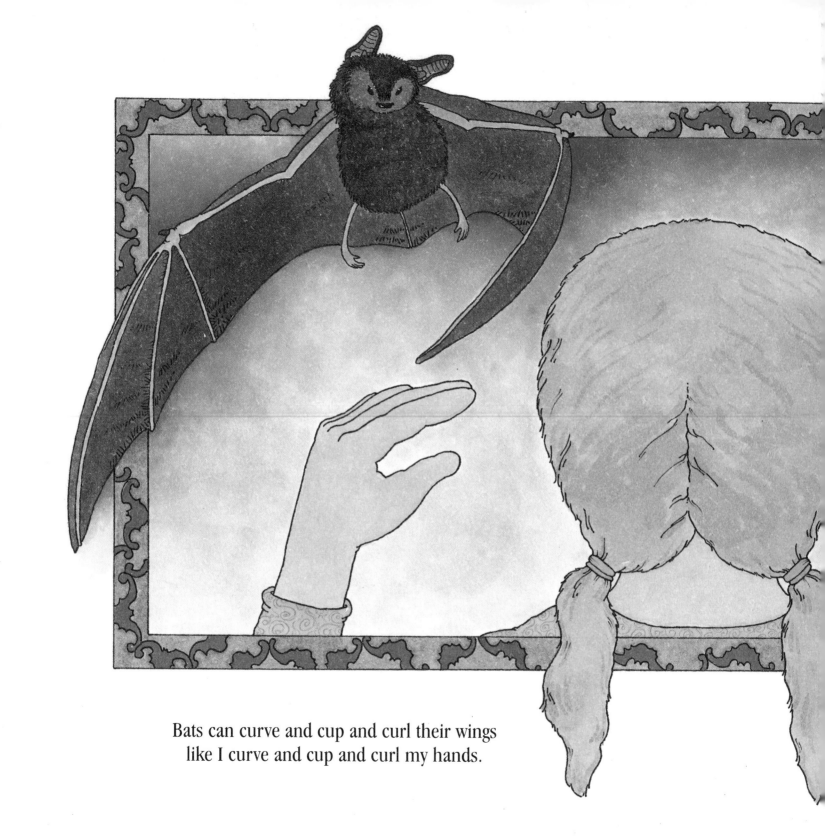

Bats can curve and cup and curl their wings
like I curve and cup and curl my hands.

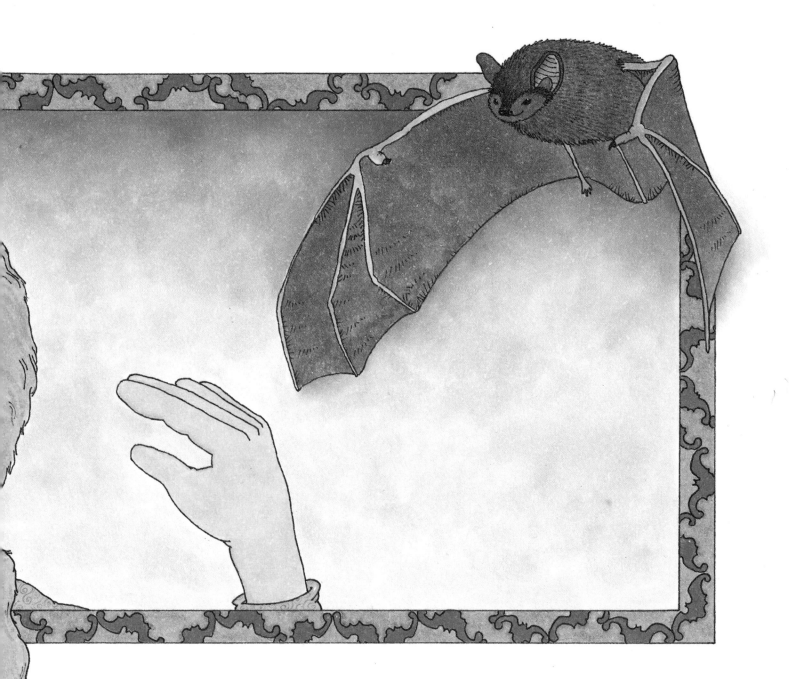

And when bats fly, they shape their wings
to swoop and soar and dart and dive.

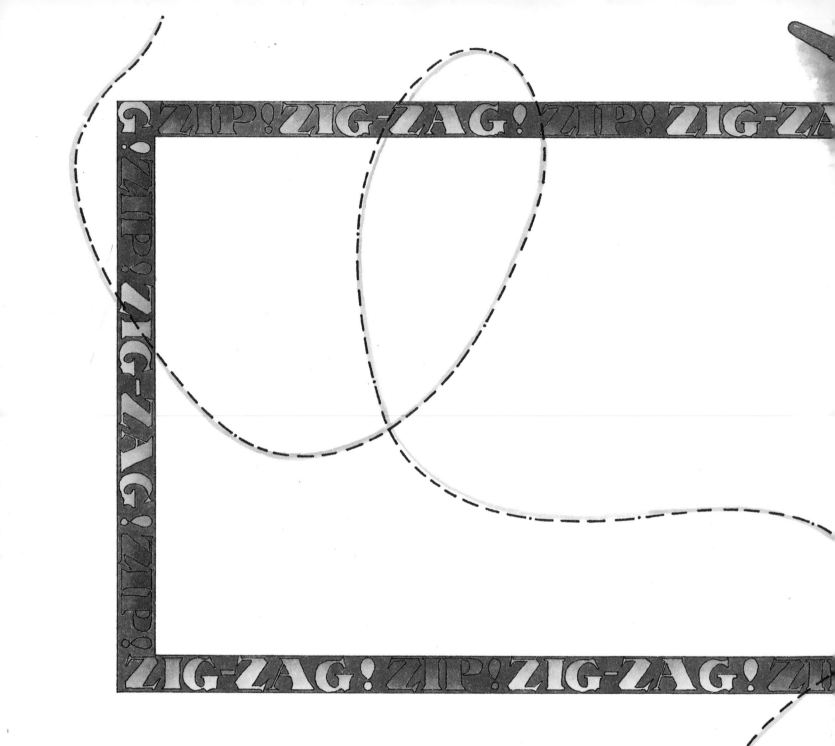

They zip and zigzag through the air

swirling spirals in the sky.

Little Brown Bats sleep during the day, hanging upside down from their toes.

Their wings look like tiny umbrellas that are neatly folded closed.

They sleep inside caves or hollow trees, in empty attics or wooden bat houses.

When my dinner is done and the sky grows dark,
all the Little Brown Bats are just waking up.

They fly out of their roosts and into the air,
flitting in and out of sight.

They zip and swoop and dart and dive,
hunting for little bugs to eat.

They catch hundreds of mosquitoes and
other bugs, and they eat them as they fly.

How do they move so fast in the dark
without bumping into things?

To zip around in the black of night,
they use their ears and their voices.

They click-click-click and chatter and chirp.

Then they listen for the echoes of their calls.

They follow the echoes of their click-click-clicks
to find their way through the darkness.

But their clicks are too high for people to hear.
So all I hear is the hush of bat wings.

As I snuggle in bed and drift off to sleep,
bats are chasing mosquitoes outside in the dark.

Little Brown Bats are my nighttime friends.
They are furry and gentle and shy.

They're the best bug-catchers of the night
and the beautiful acrobats of the sky.

Beautiful
BATS
facts

Do bats have real wings?

Yes. Bats are the only animals with both fur and wings. They are the only mammals with wings. Although flying squirrels have skin flaps that help them glide, bats are the only mammals that can truly fly.

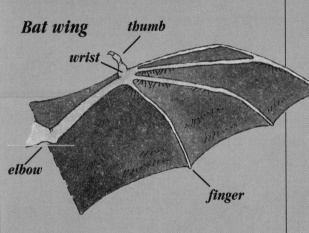

Bat wing — *thumb*, *wrist*, *elbow*, *finger*

Are bats rodents?

No. Bats are so different from any other mammal that they are given their own scientific order, called *Chiroptera*, which means "hand wing." Even humans don't have their own scientific order.

Do bats have lots of babies like mice and rats?

No. Little Brown Bats (and most other bats) have only one baby a year. This is one reason why it's so important to protect bats. They multiply very slowly.

Where do they have their babies?

Little Brown Bats have their babies in colonies with other Little Brown Bat mothers in caves, old mines, hollow trees, attics, or bat houses.

How long do bats live?

Little Brown Bats can live to be 30 years old. This is a very long time for such a small animal.

Which is the smallest bat, and which is the largest?

The Bumblebee Bat is the smallest mammal on Earth. It is about 1 inch (25 mm) long. The largest bat is the Giant Flying Fox, which is a fruit bat. It has a wingspan of about 40 inches (100 cm). Both of these bats live in the Southeast Asian rainforest.

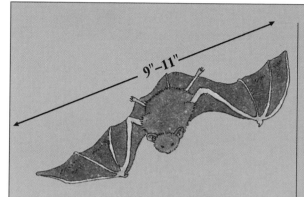

9"–11"

What size are Little Brown Bats?
Little Brown Bats are about 1 to 3 inches (25–75 mm) long, which is about the size of a field mouse or a hummingbird. But their wingspan is 9 to 11 inches (229–279 mm). So bats look much bigger in the air.

How many kinds of bats are there?
There are almost 1,000 different kinds of bats. They come in many colors—red, silver, brown, black, yellow, and white. Some have very large ears. Others have heads that look like horses, foxes, or dogs. Many are endangered.

Why do bats hang upside down?
Scientists think that bats evolved this way to take advantage of roost spaces that no other animals use—the ceilings of caves, or of hollow trees, and underneath tree branches.

Are bats blind?
No, bats can see. But most (except Flying Foxes) find their way in the dark by using their ears and voices. This is called echolocation.

Why can't people hear bats' voices?
Bats make sounds that are too high for people to hear. Another sound that's too high for people to hear is a dog whistle.

Where do bats go in the winter?

The Little Brown Bats in cold northern climates migrate to caves and abandoned mines, where they hibernate in large colonies for the winter. Most bats in northern climates migrate and hibernate. Bats in warmer climates do not.

Where on Earth do bats live?

Bats are found all over the Earth except in the Arctic and Antarctica.

Do Little Brown Bats bite people?

Little Brown Bats are shy and gentle animals. If you leave them alone, they will not bite or attack you. Most other kinds of bats are shy and gentle, too. But if a bat is hurt, sick, or cornered, it may bite in self-defense just like any other animal would.

What about Vampire Bats?

Vampire Bats are found only in Central and South America. They come out at night and find warm-blooded animals that are asleep—mainly cattle and horses, rarely people. They make a small cut and lick some blood. It's rarely harmful.

Do bats give you rabies?

Like dogs and cats, a small number of bats get rabies and can give you rabies. These bats die quickly, like any animal with rabies. If a bat is lying on the ground, stay away and leave it alone.

Who are the bats' enemies?

Hawks and owls eat Little Brown Bats. So do snakes, skunks, and cats. But people are the ones who hurt bats the most.

How do people hurt bats?

People kill whole colonies of bats because they are afraid of them. They don't know that most bats are not only harmless but are also very important.

People kill bats without knowing it. They explore caves where bats hibernate. They don't know that bats are likely to die if they are disturbed during their deep winter sleep.

People spray pesticides—insect poisons. Pesticides kill bats (and other living things) while killing the insects that bats eat.

In many places around the world, bats' habitats—the places where bats live (such as the rainforests)—are being destroyed by people.

What can people do to help bats?

Learn about bats. Most people who know about bats want to protect them and want to teach other people to protect them.

Stay away from caves where bats are rearing young or hibernating.

Become a member of Bat Conservation International. This is the only conservation group in North America that works solely to protect bats and their habitats worldwide.

Address:
Bat Conservation International (BCI)
    P.O. Box 162603
    Austin, TX 78716

Put up a bat house.

What is a bat house?

A bat house is a small box with a narrow opening on the bottom for bats to fly in and out. Thirty bats can live in one. People put them up to help protect bats. And in return, bats keep the mosquito population down. Keeping a bat house in the garden works well since bat droppings make good fertilizer. BCI sells bat houses. It also sends plans for building a bat house to donors who request them.

How many mosquitoes can one bat eat?

One Little Brown Bat can catch as many as 600 mosquitoes in one hour! They eat thousands of mosquitoes every night.

Why are bats important?

Little Brown Bats and other insect-eating bats keep the insect population down. Without bats, bothersome insects such as mosquitoes, gnats, and midges, and serious crop pests such as cucumber beetles, June bugs, stink bugs, and leaf hoppers, would quickly grow out of control.

Fruit-eating bats are important because they spread seeds and pollinate. In East Africa, the baobab tree, or the "tree of life," needs bats for its pollination. Without fruit-eating bats, whole systems of nature might collapse.

Bats are very important to our Earth, and they need to be protected.

ABOUT THE AUTHOR AND ARTIST

Linda Glaser is the author of two other Millbrook science picture books: *Wonderful Worms* and *Compost! Growing Gardens From Your Garbage*. Both books were selected as Outstanding Science Trade Books for Children by the National Science Teacher's Association/Children's Book Council. She lives in Duluth, Minnesota.

Sharon Lane Holm lives in New Fairfield, Connecticut, where she works full time as a free-lance illustrator. She has illustrated a number of Millbrook nonfiction books, among them *Nature in Your Backyard* and *Sidewalk Games Around the World*. She is also the illustrator of two highly acclaimed craft series, Holiday Crafts for Kids and Crafts for Kids Who Are Wild About.